MENTORING YOUR CHILD TO WIN

The 7 Breakthrough Keys

How A Single, Former Welfare Mom Raised A Multi-Millionaire Kid

By Arlene Karian
"The Parenting Mentor"

MENTORING YOUR CHILD TO WIN: The 7 Breakthrough Keys – How A Single, Former Welfare Mom Raised A Multi-Millionaire Kid, Copyright © 2013, by Arlene Karian. Published by LifePath Books, P.O. Box 761, Summerville, SC 29484. All rights reserved. No part of this book may be reproduced or transmitted in any form or by any means, electronic or mechanical, including photography, recording or in any information storage or retrieval system, without written permission from the author and publisher.

NOTE: This book is *not* a substitute for psychotherapy, counseling, or other professional services and it is in no way written or published to serve as such.

Print Edition

Some parents lose themselves in the parenting process.

Parenting is how I found myself.

Dedication

It is with great love that I dedicate this book to my sister, Marian Marmon, whose unfulfilled life potential served as a catalyst for this message. I equally dedicate it to children, parents, and persons who seek to experience the full panorama of their gifts.

—Arlene Karian, 2013

Acknowledgements

Aside from the gift of my son, there are others who brought balm to my body, mind, and spirit in some way along my journey. I acknowledge them here.

To my father, for his dedication to excellence, culture and values.

To my mother, whose musical and poetic gifts – along with her sense of beauty – were her legacy to me.

To my sister Marian, for whom this book is dedicated. I miss our childhood giggles and the years of bonding that we lost.

To Professor Trippepi, whose country home and sprawling patio was a perfect backdrop for my first piano lessons.

To Professor Rudko and Dean Allen Verhines, for the generosity of their time, teaching, and faith in my vocal talent.

To my early California experience, where music and sun lighted my way.

Arlene Karian

To my first vocal teacher, Florence Holbrook, who taught me that music and spirituality *do* co-exist.

To Bill and Brian, who were both there for me at different crises points in my life, helping me without asking for anything in return.

To Erik LaMont, for sweeping me into the romance of a lifetime, teaching me about navigating life effectively, and confirming to me that my values were the only foundation for my life.

To Anna, for the many gifts of your friendship, including teaching me about unconditional caring.

To Michael, who left too soon. My dearest soul-friend who, with an uncommon selflessness, fed my mind and spirit for 30 years. You left me with so much of your gifts. Be in peace.

To Thurman, for being Stephan's counselor and role model, and for imprinting him with the spiritual side of the male; whose spiritual genius taught me the value of releasing pain and negativity. Also for opening me up to the different sides of myself.

To Sheri Levitus, who helped put me back together when I was lost, and who has charted and *is* charting my journey with me to this day. Thank you for being there for me.

To Tony Robbins, whose commitment to high functioning and indefatigable service to others has been my son's early guiding light and role model.

To Ali Yassin, for infusing my son with values, goals, and passion.

To Ava and Ethan, my grandchildren, who are flourishing into young adulthood with the freedom and expert guidance to explore their true nature.

To Marty and Shelly, my brother and sister-in-law, whose warm hearth filled our hungry bodies and souls during Stephans' formative years.

To my four soul pets, Lucky, Smudge, Baby Girl, and Sammie. You opened a museum of feelings that no other beings could and charged my soul with indescribable and unduplicatable love. Thank you for that. And – Sammie – thank you for being in my life now.

To Lori Karian, my daughter-in-law, who showed me that you can be "deep" and also have fun and enjoy your life.

To Pat and Joe Abruzzo, whose warm hospitality always makes me feel downright good and special.

To my three life-changing coaches, in order of their appearance in my life.

Arlene Karian

To Sam Horn, who comes from another planet and brings with her an outrageous spin on how to get attention.

To Sharon Wilson, my special coach who gave me the expert guidance and foundation that shaped my work. My deep affection and admiration go to you. I will cherish the memories of what we accomplished together.

To James Malinchak, who appeared on ABC's hit TV Show, *Secret Millionaire*. He hammered out the outline for this book in his Las Vegas home.

To Garth, whose outstretched hand has always been there, with or without a crisis.

To every "accident" that got my attention and *always* opened up a brighter window.

To all the doctors and practitioners who pulled me back from the edge and repaired my wings, so I could resume my life work. I have much, much gratitude for you in my life and I am in awe of your gifts.

To Elizabeth Ayres, who in a dimmed parlor in New York City 20 years ago, pricked opened up the capsule to my creative writing, and named me a "word Shaman". I humbly thank you.

And to all those unmentioned who brushed against my life.

You have all left me forever changed.

I love you.

And, finally:
To the *Mystery*, for honoring me
with a key that helped me
navigate this bumpy mortal road.

—Arlene Karian, 2013

Table of Contents

Dedication v
Acknowledgements vii
Introduction xv

Part 1 1

Why This Book is Different 3
Why Parenting Methods Throughout the Ages Have Not Been Enough – and Why The Need for this Innovative Perspective is Greater Than Ever 9
Old Ways 17
New Ways 19

Part 2 21

My Story: How a Single Mother on Welfare Raised a Son Who Became a Multi-Millionaire 23
Taking Stock, Taking Steps 27
What Was I *Really* Facing? 35
Stephan's Story *Parts 1–8* 39

Part 3: Your New Blueprint for Raising Extraordinary Kids 65

- Key #1: If You Want Something You Never Had, You Have To Do Something You Never Did 67
- Key #2: Getting Centered, Staying Centered: Creating New Habits for Better Results 69

- Key #3: Aligning with What Really Matters To You – Living In Your Values Zone 85
- Key #4: Easing Into Mentorship – Parenting for the 21st Century 93
- Key #5: Experiencing the Light: Life on a Brighter Level...113
- Key #6: Living in the Light: Using and Sharing the Radiance 117
- Key #7: Automatic Cruise Control: Navigating Your Days with Joy and Ease 123
- Epilogue 127
- Meet Arlene Karian..131

Introduction

This is a book about a journey that began with a parent and a child and the powerful natural connection between them, singular in its fierceness, instinctive protectiveness, and potentially one of the deepest forms of love. I hope to reveal to you how I found an innovative way to parent my child so he would experience an extraordinary life, and to show you how you can do the same.

The journey begins with parenting, but it's also about healing: healing for those who are not just parents or children; healing for anyone who wants a better life. It includes a daily healing process, for those who no longer want to settle for less than the best life has to offer, and for those who are tired of searching – but not finding – answers that will guide them to live the lives they *want* to live. I was a divorced single mother on welfare when I chose to assume the sole guardianship of my young son. Within me burned a deep passion to cultivate the best in him, so he'd have the skills and tools to create the kind of life for himself he dreamed of living. I wanted this for his children, too – empowering a new generation of people ready to face any economic, social, political, and environmental challenges that beset us in this 21st century, and any unknown challenges of the future.

In searching for answers, I stumbled upon a way to do exactly this. It became so incredibly exciting, so powerful and yet so natural, that my son's upbringing became a work of art.

My son's subsequent success as a young businessman and as a contributor to other people's lives led me to broaden my outreach. I now hope to reach not only parents and guardians who have the delicate and sacred charge of helping shape a child's life, but also grandparents who co-parent, and anyone else eager to contribute their gifts to change the world for the better. By embracing this journey, anyone can truly experience the simultaneous miracle of amplifying their own spiritual capacities by achieving the self-fulfillment and joy that comes from helping others. I sincerely want you to be able to experience this, too.

Through the incredible voyage of mentoring my son, my surprise gift has been the revelation of the most expansive version of myself *and* my son – as we navigated through the rich labyrinth of our lives together.

Many years after I developed this system, I was delighted and deeply gratified to learn of the breakthrough research of Dr. Robert Epstein, one of the world's leading psychologists and former editor of *Psychology Today* magazine.

At the 2010 annual meeting of the American Psychological Association, Dr. Epstein gave the results of his study involving over 2000 parents. The outcome of this critical, groundbreaking report was validated by elaborate statistical analysis and by the review of over 50 prior studies on this subject to refine the research methodology used by Dr. Epstein and his team, in order to arrive at the best possible ways to investigate this crucial topic with absolute accuracy.

Of the top three factors linked to successful parenting, two of them were *not* solely related to what the parent does or says to the child. Instead, they consisted of the parent incorporating the following into all aspects of his or her life—not just parenting:

    (a) Well-developed stress management abilities, and

    (b) Good relationship skills. The single most important factor of the three – <u>giving the child lots of love and affection</u> – will obviously be a difficult challenge for the parent to consistently provide if the parent isn't competent in stress management and good relationship skills.

Dr. Epstein's research discovered that, unfortunately, most parents are decidedly substandard in these areas. The system provided in this book *will* change that factor, empowering you as a parent to raise the bar in these and other critical areas of everyday life. As a result, when you choose this method, you *will* ultimately raise extraordinary children who will be empowered to make positive choices and who will experience extraordinary lives; the lives they were *meant* to live.

Part 1

Why This Book is Different

Current parenting methods and models are *not* working. In fact, it's always been this way, but they work much less now, with the enormous challenges we face in today's society. This book – and the system I developed through my own experience – represents a truly revolutionary breakthrough in the parenting process.

Here's why:

It goes beyond all root assumptions about *any* and *all* parenting approaches. The parental guidance given by well-meaning authors has plenty of merit. However, through no fault of their own, their directives were voiced without the fundamental prerequisites I've discovered and reveal in this book.

This model, *unlike any other*, does not focus on the child or on the parents' relationship with him or her. Instead, it focuses on parental self-development, so the parent – by consistently and systematically raising their consciousness – becomes a living role model, positively affecting the behavior and consciousness of the child, eliciting the child's highest self as a result. It's about developing the ability to access, understand, and utilize one's own consciousness—expanding and integrating it into everyday life so that it governs all aspects of your being, in *addition* to your parenting. As a result, you'll have an ongoing customized life plan for yourself, based on your individual uniqueness, with an emphasis on high ethical and moral values.

It's also about positive fundamental change and recognizing and manifesting one's true life-path. My system shows you how to handle your whole life in general and the relationship with your child from an entirely new perspective of *mentorship*.

It helps to develop positive stress management and relationship abilities in new ways, and it raises one's own personal effectiveness and personal power simultaneously to an extent you might not have dreamt possible.

This book provides you with the specific technology that teaches you how to do this.

This shift through parental self-development will dramatically improve *any* parent-child relationship, because parents who experience it will be looking at *every* aspect of their own lives in a different, more elevated manner. This will naturally result in newly uplifted ways of thinking and feeling about their children.

Until now, parents have had no choice but to constantly be "putting out fires," reacting and responding to whatever happens with or involving the child. My process, however, actually puts you into a far more coherent, ongoing, uplifted psychological state. As a result, your perspective becomes more evolved and the child benefits immeasurably, even though the interaction might be completely non-verbal.

Parents are, as a result, able to become role models and mentors, relating to their children more effectively and positively. This naturally brings forth both the child's and the parents' greatest potential.

- My process is non-religious and non-theological, designed to be acceptable to almost anyone. Participants don't have to "buy into" any belief system other than their own values, supported by the framework of universal truths.
- The basic premise of this process remedies the absence of a fundamental knowledge, perspective, and wisdom that's been the norm throughout the ages. This premise was scientifically validated decades after I created it.
- This process does more than simply fill the need to raise our consciousness in order to cope with all the difficulties in our lives and the world. ***It also provides the technology to make the necessary changes.*** It intercepts and reverses a degeneration that can easily occur if we become overwhelmed by the negativity we're constantly bombarded with in our daily lives.

- Because this process is interactive, a customized/tailored roadmap will emerge based on your individual values, personality, lifestyle, religion, and spiritual path or tradition.
- The depth of the process creates fundamental positive change in the ways you would want and choose to live your life.
- It elicits your unique contributions and enables you to do the same for your child/children.
- It develops your ability to both create and sustain a higher state of consciousness on a daily basis – easily and naturally.
- It facilitates your actions and decisions to naturally emerge from your core values, enabling you to stay on track instead of being constantly derailed by knee-jerk reactions.
- My process provides a roadmap for each day and evolves from consistency, following the directions provided in this simple system.
- The work is solidly based on the values that underlie civilization and that are reflected in the great religions and the writings of the major philosophers.
- Because this process emphasizes ethics and moral values, it goes beyond just the individual's needs, desires, and agenda. As you become aligned with your own "personal truths" and act in accordance with them – experiencing the fulfillment of living within your own values, in the

process – you organically begin to reach out in contribution to your children and to others.

- I'm excited to share my discovery with you. It's my sincere hope that parents, teachers, guardians, aunts, uncles, grandmothers, grandfathers – anyone who is involved in shaping the life of a child – will see this book as a new way to awaken their highest potential and become a catalyst for raising an extraordinary child.

Our world is waiting for it. Our world is ready for it.

Then everything – yes, <u>everything</u> – will change.

I remember the day I started having labor pains from my son. We had to move fast, as they were becoming more frequent. We rushed to the elevator on the eleventh floor in our apartment building, only to find an "Out of Order" sign on the door.

I couldn't believe this was happening – at a time like this! There was no way I could get down eleven flights of stairs in my current condition, so we took the service elevator and found ourselves crammed inside, sharing the space with tons of black plastic bags of garbage collected from eleven floors! I looked at the numbers as we passed each floor: 10-9-8-7-... all while the labor pains were becoming more frequent and intense.

Suddenly, I looked at the lifeless garbage around me and I was hit by the contrast of it to the impending birth of my child. I made a vow right then and there – just before the next labor pain – that my child would <u>never</u> have to experience the struggle and lack that I was experiencing in my life and confronting at that moment. I pledged to make it my mission to (a) raise a successful, outstanding human being who would also make a difference in people's lives, and (b) create my own personal prosperity in the process.

That is – <u>if</u> it were up to me.

I learned it was – and that vow burned in my belly. Eventually, it resulted in this book.

Why Parenting Methods Throughout the Ages Have Not Been Enough – and Why The Need for this Innovative Perspective is Greater Than Ever

Good parents are everywhere: PTA meetings, ballgames, school dances, camps, and supermarkets. All well-meaning parents feel the same when their children are born. They want the best for them. They'll give them their best advice, care, and love.

Many parents make tremendous sacrifices when raising their children. But – through no fault of their own – the results have often been, at a minimum, not good enough. As a result, our children have become too vulnerable to negative outside influences.

What's missing? Why are parenting methods not working in this regard? For the answers, we'll need to look at two universes, so to speak: the outer world and the inner world of our thoughts, which result in the actions we take.

Let's first look at the outer world. What's going on out there in the outside world?

We're going through unprecedented political, social, and environmental changes. We are constantly bombarded by bank crises, terrorist attacks, sovereign debt crises, climate change worries, food shortages, and ecological woes.

Parents are forced to face new challenges – there's less human interaction due to the explosion of the digital age; increases in bullying and teen suicides; and levels of violence have escalated in movies, television, and video games. Recently, on CNN, a teenager who killed his parents warned people who are troubled to avoid looking at violent video games. He believed that, in his case, the violence he watched increased and escalated the desire to commit his subsequent act of murder.

The availability of world-wide news has accelerated the viewing of negative, stressful world events instantly as they happen. We're fed negativity as quickly as fast food, with the same unhealthy consequences – one affecting our bodies, the other affecting our minds and emotions.

In addition, the media is manipulating our perceptions of what's real or not real with programs being referred to as "reality TV."

Amidst these political, social, and environmental changes we're all experiencing, parents often feel confused, overwhelmed, and "stuck" because of this constant rapid flux and chaos in the world.

Often, we don't know where to turn for advice – or the answers we *do* get are insufficient to help solve our current challenges. On top of that, many parents feel they have no time to breathe, and they are stressed out with the increasing demands the current frantic pace of life imposes upon them. This accelerated pace of life has increased the demands on all of us and has brought with it 21st century exhaustion. Small wonder many parents feel frazzled.

How about you?

Dr. Oz has called this the "Exhaustion Age," and I believe he's correct in his characterization of this time in history.

Now, let's talk about our *inner* world – the one that deals with our thoughts and feelings.

How does this pace of life affect our parenting? As parents, we absorb the pressures, concerns, and fears of the outside world and our decisions are filtered through that perspective into our daily lives. *Our perspective is the most important influencing factor shaping the growth and formation of our children.* We unwittingly transfer that perspective – whatever it may be – directly to them every single day.

So, along with unprecedented pressures of daily life and chaos in the world, the parenting models, as they currently stand, are clearly not meeting the challenges of current times. We're running the "business" of parenting by the seat of our pants, constantly putting out fires rather than setting positive precedents and establishing more effective ways of child rearing.

Unfortunately, a new paradigm based on a proper foundation – parental self-development – has not been available up to this point.

How does the current out-of-date parenting modality affect our children?

Since our children are the direct recipients of our influence on them, *both* parents *and* children are clearly being exposed to challenges never before dealt with in history. Your children are feeling it right along with you. The onslaught of 21st century problems and challenges – along with the resulting impact of outside negative influences – are more than just a deep concern for parents. Current conditions have, in fact, only highlighted the need for a new, dependable parenting model that can stand up to the times we live in now.

The basic problem has been the fact that the ways we've parented throughout history have lacked a firm foundation in what's now referred to as an expanded awareness. The various attempts at designing different forms of parenting through the ages have all lacked an essential basic reference point that's never before been articulated. That is, they lacked a systematic technology showing the parent how to access, evoke, and implement a higher level of consciousness and functioning that's **directly applied to all aspects of the parents' lives, <u>including</u> parenting itself**.

Our contemporary challenges now *demand* taking a quantum leap to fill this long-standing vacuum. Children previously looked to celebrity role models for guidance. Now, they see them in courtrooms on TV. It's become commonplace to watch many celebrities – former beacons of respect and admiration – as they publicly battle their demons without a strong inner self to lean on. The disappointment in those thought to be role models or those looking for role models in the wrong places has all but distorted our core values and led our youth to rationalize their own ill-chosen actions and – on the worst end of the scale – to violate the law.

A child's cynicism, lack of respect, and feelings of worthlessness can be a distorted response to the questions, "Who am I?" "Why am I here?" and "Where am I going?"

These legitimate questions leave our children vulnerable when they're not properly answered. The vacuum this creates may be filled with the wrong answers. In the absence of an anchor, stability, or appropriate role models, our children – through the need to find answers to fill the vacuum – seek a sense of connection and they far too often now look to get their kicks in the wrong places. They commonly seek those answers in sexual promiscuity, bullying and other violence, teen pregnancies, drugs, racism, and in an "us versus them" mentality.

In addition, the digital age threatens to take away any shred of human interaction and connectedness. This has dramatically added to the challenges of current parenting models.

Just recently, I saw a four-year-old lunching with her mother. They were looking at their respective "smart" phones throughout the entire meal. There was *no* connection between them throughout their time together, and this has become more commonplace.

With a distorted foundation and a lack of eye-to-eye connection with loved ones, where does this leave our youth?

What if there was a parenting model that would work, no matter *what* changed in society or in the future – no matter *what* new technology or world event came along?

The **7 Keys**, explored in Part 3 of this book, will fill that vacuum and open the door to integrating this new paradigm of expanded awareness into both the parenting process and into what will also become your own uplifted life.

This is the *new* parenting model.

Parents: If you feel you've not accomplished effective child rearing, or if you fear you're failing, I want you to know *it's not your fault!*

Because of the way the world and mass culture impinges on both children and families, we clearly need to raise our thinking to another level in order to obtain different solutions to these challenges. As mentioned above, the current state of the world has clearly brought about challenges never before encountered in daily life – challenges making our lives increasingly complex. At a basic level, the ethical, moral, and spiritual values common to the great religions, to the major secular philosophical writings, and to the universal values that underlie civilization and give guidance and meaning to life, haven't been learned and incorporated. They've instead been systematically neglected or violated on a very grand scale – not only by individuals but by powerful institutions as well.

Since these values represent time-honored concepts of what's right and, therefore, *needed* for happiness in individual lives and for the good of society itself, it's not surprising most of mankind's present problems are a direct result of breaching them.

Consequently, many of our youth today are dealing with a lack or loss of meaning in their lives. The core values that have helped families and children connect and create abundant lives have all too often become obscured under the rubble of contemporary chaos. Is it any wonder that our children have made negative choices?

Holistic "win/win" solutions that comply with universal values both exist and are constantly emerging – but they're not yet in predominance. This work and my system will accelerate that trend by changing the consciousness of both the parent *and* child. This new state of consciousness will help them make their individual contributions to society...and to each other.

Though every age has its unique challenges, I want to reassure you we have the power to change the way we think – the ways that were foisted upon us, even in our current crisis, and to allow a new perspective to filter into every life we shape, regardless of what's going on in the world.

The exciting news is that it can change – *now*.

I did it and so can you. In the following pages, I'll show you how.

Old Ways

Let's first touch on the "Old Ways" of parenting – or the more traditional forms – and why those ways didn't work then and aren't working today.

Modern psychology, as we understand it, began from the middle-to-late 1800's. Before – and certainly since that time – much has been written about parenting guidelines and child-rearing. Between the extremes – of "spare the rod, spoil the child" and "Tiger Mom," (current research, in *Slate* Magazine, 2013, has validated negative results from this latter form of parenting), to permissiveness, "be a pal to your child," and the most recent writings about "intuitive parenting," or "attachment parenting" – much has changed. Many psychological assumptions have been made and acted upon by writers and parents alike, with much merit in many cases – but they all lacked the indispensable foundation of expanded awareness, or what is referred to as higher consciousness.

New Ways

Now – let's talk about the new ways: what's needed in today's society for children *and* adults:

Einstein tells us that you can't solve a problem from the same place that the problem arose.

What if, as a parent, you discovered all the answers to parenting were within your reach **– by raising, as Einstein suggests, your "level of thinking?"**

What if you also found that the secret to rearing a great child included becoming the best version of *yourself?*

Let me tell you how I discovered that to be true.

Part 2

My Story: How a Single Mother on Welfare Raised a Son Who Became a Multi-Millionaire

In 1967, I gave birth to my son. Like many new parents, I was committed to giving him my very best. However, when he was six months old, I made the decision to separate from my husband.

I'd experienced enough traumas during our short marriage to seriously question the integrity of the man I'd married. Not wanting my child to grow up in the crossfire of an unhappy and divided home, I decided to end the marriage and resolved to raise my son myself.

After my husband was asked to leave our home, he would make appointments for visitation rights and not show up. I can still remember the letdown feeling of arriving with my son, very early in the morning, at an appointed place – sometimes in the cold of winter – only to wait for a long time before realizing that his father wasn't going to show up.

As a result of this repeated behavior, a judge suspended his visitation rights permanently and awarded me sole custody. In an act of spite, my husband refused to support us from that point forward.

In a very short time, I was faced with poverty *and* sole guardianship. I was very frightened, as financial pressures and my larger responsibility to the child I loved deeply were now uppermost on my mind. I turned to my family for assistance. They didn't agree with my decision to raise my child alone, so I didn't have the support of relatives during that early plight. In fact, they suggested I put my son up for adoption! My family seemed disappointed in the direction they felt my life had taken. The pursuit of a musical career – one I'd worked so long and hard to develop – had come to a halt.

I swallowed the hurt and lack of support, crying alone many nights.

Fatigue, loneliness, anxiety, and overwhelming fear were my unwelcome companions during those early years. I faced the same daily challenges many parents do, but mine were compounded by single parenthood. Many single parents might identify with some of the challenges I faced.

After the separation, I was lonely and friendless, having gone from a single-life-culture to a married-life-culture, then to a socially unacceptable divorced-single-mother-culture – all within a year. The process of being a new mother alone is an identity shift. With all the other upheavals in my life, including no financial support, I was distraught. My mother never offered to take me in and didn't offer monetary help. The family wanted to see us for visits, but no one was about to open their doors to me and actually ask, "How can I support you? What do you need? How can I help?"

Taking Stock, Taking Steps

I remember looking at my sleeping child in his crib one day, thinking, "This is truly a sacred charge. My little boy depends on me for his sustenance in every way: food, love, nurturing, protection, safety, guidance, and education."

I remember that moment as clearly as if it happened yesterday. The love and commitment I felt was stronger than my struggle for survival and personal identity.

Good, well-meaning parents know this feeling well. As I watched him sleep, a feeling of helplessness overcame me. Would I be able to take on the responsibility of being a single parent? Did I really have the "stuff?"

I didn't know where to turn. I didn't even know if there were answers. Ready or not, the time came for me to move forward. Physical survival was first.

A neighbor in my apartment building suggested I immediately get on welfare. Though I found it humiliating at first, it certainly felt better to be able to feed both myself and my child. Yet, I still felt desperate and alone—pulled in a direction where I knew none of the rules. The only thing I could be sure of was uncertainty. For me, there was nowhere else to turn to for solace but inward. On an instinctive level, I felt I would find direction there.

The first step I took was to look into myself – to my own spirituality – for self-nourishment.

Each of us has a personal choice to find or create a spiritual place within ourselves. Though it's different for all of us, it is within all of us. For me, it was critical that I find and create that space, because I felt there was nowhere else to turn.

I wondered: Where did I fit in the world?

My personal identity had suddenly changed when I became a parent. I was no longer a carefree single woman pursuing a musical career. I was the guardian of a child and I felt totally committed to giving him my best and wanted to better our lives.

Right before my son was born, I had a rare opportunity for a coveted Metropolitan Opera audition. However, during this time it was commonly accepted that you needed to have another type of talent as well – and it wasn't singing. It was excelling at a "couch interview."

I refused.

Though I'd worked long and hard to develop my singing and musicianship skills, the stand I took at that time was a forerunner to an allegiance to my values. I had to face my life now in its present circumstances, and deep within me I had no doubt that whatever the future held, those early values would be upheld and honored.

So there I was: a brand new mom, all alone with my son. It was a time when I knew I had to function differently. There were many questions, but no answers for me "out there." You have to understand: this was the late 60's and early 70's. The world was a different place. Being divorced with a child was a scary situation to be in and not nearly as common as it is today. There was a stigma attached not only to being a single woman, but also to any single woman raising a child alone. If there were support groups for women like me, I was unaware of them at the time. Along with the insecurities about my newly responsible, yet unfamiliar role, I felt I had *nowhere* to go for help.

Although there wasn't an economic meltdown going on right then, I felt I was in my own private one. In terms of supporting myself, there was no way for me to get a "real" job, because the only thing I was good at was singing. Or so I thought at the time. Unlike today, books explaining the pregnancy process, such as *What to Expect When You're Expecting*, didn't exist. I felt isolated, inexperienced, and – as far as I knew – there was nothing out there to support me, because my situation wasn't common or accepted. Despite my dire circumstances, I was still determined to create a better life for my son. Little did I realize at the time, that I would be blazing a new trail both for myself and for others.

The years I'd spent crafting my art as a singer/musician afforded me no business work experience. I also had to get childcare if I was to work – and, at that time, my primary concern was having enough money to feed us, not paying for any additional expenses.

Had I known what I learned later, and am sharing with you here, life would have been *much* easier. However, I realized later in my life that I was meant to pioneer this work, so others could benefit from it.

Soon, I was led to read books that made me feel better, that fed my soul and uplifted me. I read *The Bible*; *Man's Search for Meaning,* by Victor Frankel; *Siddhartha,* by Herman Hesse; *Saint Francis,* by Nikos Kazantzakis; and *Meditation for Children,* by Deborah Rozman. I later realized that these choice books contained philosophical wisdom – moral and ethical values that have been upheld throughout the ages and that, therefore, contain universally applicable truths. I was deeply drawn to these books that inspired me and gave me solace. I sensed that, beneath me, I was weaving a foundation that had begun to grow and would take shape, grounding me for the road ahead.

I had my first paradigm shift – an "aha moment" – after being led to a woman who lived across the street. I found out she would give free advice for anyone who couldn't afford it, so I headed over with my son in his carriage and I told her what I was going through. I remember asking her for advice that would keep my two feet on the ground and improve my life.

She asked me, "How's this? What are your initials?" I replied, "A - S - K," and she said, "That is all you ever have to do: ASK."

"Was it really that easy?" I thought. What strange advice to give a desperate woman! Without taking it seriously, I filed it somewhere in my mind, more concerned with my feelings of desperation with my daily challenges at the time than I was about figuring out exactly what she meant.

To my credit, I'd already made choices about my life on a values basis that came to me naturally. I didn't choose alcohol, drugs, anger, or cavorting around to solve my problems.

I loved my son completely and I wanted a better life for us. When I left that woman's house that day, though I had no immediate answers for my day-to-day life, something must have been born in me of which I was unaware. I left her apartment knowing I *had* to begin somewhere, but I still didn't feel I had an answer. Little did I know, her advice would turn into a path that would change the course of my entire life.

One providential morning, as natural as breathing, I turned inward and began a journey of "asking" that eventually led me to find the answer I was looking for all along – *me*. What seemed to develop, almost *organically* after that, was an early morning practice that helped me begin to feel balanced and provided me with a daily structure. It gave my life direction. This single act would come to be my life's path and lead to my own and to my son's success.

I want to differentiate this early morning practice from what one might conclude was a religious quest, as this wasn't the case. I was actually seeking a personal identity and I was led, as a result, to setting aside quiet time to explore ME. I was at the beginning of my journey to find new answers to old questions. I made a commitment to become fit with my mind, with my brain, and with my consciousness – much in the same way that we make a commitment to be fit by giving our bodies what they need. I realized, if I wanted a new life, then – according to Einstein – I would have to go to a different level of functioning than the one that had brought me to divorce, poverty, and single motherhood.

When I "went inside," I found that my heart and mind had many undiscovered rooms. I was able to get access to these new places – where I began to develop a whole new set of inner muscles.

That's when I started to change my perspective *and* my actions.

I started finding direction and – yes – answers. As I shifted my thinking, I noticed I was making better decisions and I felt empowered to rise above my challenges. I also noticed the negativity surrounding my life was slowly being replaced by joy, hope, and confidence.

I was beginning to see that this new perspective was more than just about my son. It was about becoming the best version of *me*, so I could set a different kind of example to the child I would help form, raise, grow, support, and – eventually – mentor. My commitment to changing my life led me to reach a deep understanding that the life I had been leading was a result of choices I made, and as I learned to access new, expanded abilities and make *new* choices, my life turned around. I also developed the ability to become my son's mentor.

When you understand this process, it'll become indispensable in your life. The purity and balance underlying this system and its natural existing inherence in us all will make it easy to access, learn, and apply.

Each of us has a personal choice to find or create a spiritual place within ourselves and nurture it. The search, if we're blessed enough to desire it, is different for all of us. But, in the end, what we're all looking for instinctively is wholeness.

For me, it was critical that I find and create that space, because I felt there was nowhere else for me to go. I wondered: Where did I fit in the world? My personal identity had suddenly changed when I became a parent. With that change, so did my priorities.

My greatest challenge now would be finding answers that would prepare my child to be safe while flourishing in this society, in spite of my present circumstances. Turning inward helped to sort out my thinking and ground me for what might lie ahead.

As I relied upon and trusted my inner practice more and more, I eventually felt I was ready to venture outward for answers. My body and my spirit were getting the attention they needed. I now had to use my mind to test the outside waters of our culture and environment. Ready or not, I had to turn outward and move forward.

What Was I *Really* Facing?

As an idealist whose background was in the arts and humanities, this was a new and strange world for me. In addition to a singing career, mentioned previously, I'd also spent the greater part of my early years being lauded as a child prodigy on the piano. After my son's birth, I willingly gave up my musical career and considered the guardianship of my son as my ultimate work of art. Fortunately, although I was no longer pursuing a career in the arts, my background enabled me to bring both creativity and sensitivity to parenting.

However, over the following years, I was challenged to use *both* sides of my brain: the creative *and* the analytical. This was not easy for me, as I'd always considered myself an artist.

Venturing out of the familiar confines of the creative personality made me explore other aspects of my thinking process. In doing so, I stretched new mental muscles that helped me engineer innovative ways of approaching parenthood.

Turning outward to look at the world around me, at the time when my little boy was about three years old, I asked myself, "Where do I begin? How do I start?"

Totally unaware of the pitfalls that lay ahead, I began looking at the ways our environment shapes our children: our schools, the mass media, peer groups, and unconscious parental influence. I found that the educational system wasn't providing the stimuli for children to think creatively or to successfully navigate the shoals of youth and adolescence. Our teachers were – and still are – overworked, under-appreciated, and their idealism continually put to an acid test. It seemed none of those channels that influence our children were supplying answers. Instead, they were projecting negativity, fear, and insecurity.

Mass media, peer groups, and the educational system were a reflection of the major trends of our culture. They presented a mixed bag of shadows that loomed over me, splaying themselves across the decades of the 60's and 70's. The openness of the 60's brought our puritanical and repressed society out from hiding. Popular Eastern and homegrown gurus advocated meditation and looking "inside" for the answers. Dr. Timothy Leary's admonition, to "Turn on, tune in and drop out," was the mantra that invited breaking rules and/or dropping out of society for many young people. It also provided a green light to go beyond the constricted parameters of the former culture. Drugs, the sexual revolution, the revolt against the "Establishment," and the Vietnam War – all promoted protests and alienation. The movement toward euphoria and away from responsibility added to the swirling currents that echoed through the fast-moving years of the late 60's into the mid 70's.

A profound alienation, cynicism, and disappointment regarding the then-current political, social, and economic structure and ideology prevailed—fueled by the assassinations of John F. Kennedy, Robert F. Kennedy, and Martin Luther King Jr. With Watergate, followed by Nixon's resignation, the American people had lost their innocence.

In the midst of this over-arching upheaval, all I could think about was: how could I culture-proof my child and protect him from losing **his** innocence?

I not only found the climate for stability and direction to be shaky but also frightening. I saw a dehumanized culture that would not and could not offer a road map or rudder for life management. The challenges of parenting – then and *much* more now – were stretched way beyond the model of earlier times, and then escalated into distorted and unfamiliar territory.

Parenting – as it stood in its various forms – needed a fundamental framework from which different results would follow.

I discovered that, with the best of intentions, good parenting alone was no longer enough.

Stephan's Story
Part 1

For the moment, let's fast forward to May 19, 2000 – a day vividly etched in my memory, a day that symbolized the fruition of an incredible journey with a child placed in my hands by Providence to love, care for, nurture, and *mentor*.

Great American Products, one of the leading nutritional companies in the United States, was celebrating the opening of its expansion to a 12,000 square-foot facility in Destin, Florida that day. The event was attended by the Destin Chamber of Commerce and the Better Business Bureau – two prestigious organizations of which Great American Products is a member.

The company was – and still is – operated by Stephan Karian and his extremely capable wife, Lori. They were both in their early thirties back then, and the success and the growth of their business have been meteoric ever since the company's formation in September of 1994.

What does this have to do with mentoring as it applies to parenthood? A great deal.

Stephan Karian is my son.

Thinking back, raising Stephan alone from the age of 6 months until adulthood, without a manual or road map, expanded my ordinary capacities. The parenting factor was alive and well, as evidenced by my strong maternal love, but I soon became aware of another dynamic that was also strong – but *different*.

That dynamic was *mentoring*.

What's the difference between *parenting* and *mentoring*?

> *Oxford Dictionary Thesaurus* defines "mentor" as, "An experienced and trusted Advisor." Coach, Counselor, Guide, Guru, Instructor, Teacher, Trainer, Tutor."

As a single mother, I felt compelled to equip my child with a system of life skills that could be integrated into daily life today. My determination was a strong motivational factor and it became a daily creative act. Together with Stephan's own natural abilities, and the use of certain skills, strategies, and techniques, I armed my son with tools that would connect him to his unique personal power – ultimately, *and naturally,* weaving the foundation for his success.

In doing so, my own efforts at self-betterment were perpetuated through him, galvanizing him to utilize his own uniqueness in building his future. What resulted, in addition to parenting?

I also became my son's *mentor*.

Stephan's Story
Part 2

My commitment to help shape an extraordinary child started while my son was still in the womb. During my pregnancy, I felt directed to communicate specific messages to my child. I started watching closely the music I selected, my interaction with others, the books I read, and the thoughts I entertained.

I later learned both Dr. Varney's book, *The Secret Life Of The Unborn Child"* and Dr. Monida Lukesch's research concluded that the mother's attitude had the single greatest effect on how an infant turned out and everything the mother thought, felt, said, and hoped for influenced her unborn child. Additionally, the mother could make those thoughts have as positive an effect as she wished! I was delighted to discover had I instinctively and deliberately used this practice 35 years before the book was ever published!

I'd always loved to read – mostly books on self-growth, empowerment, and achievement. It fascinated me then – and it still does today – how anyone can create the life they desire by intention and by simply directing their minds to focus on a desired outcome. Now I was purposefully communicating positive thoughts and insights to my son during quiet, restful times.

Friend selection was a challenge for me on the streets of New York City. I had to become creative if I hoped to protect my son from bad influences that were in abundant supply and so easily accessible.

When Stephan was a pre-teen, I decided to include his friends in weekly meetings, to express their feelings and talk about what they'd like to create in their lives. I led some visualization exercises that involved making free choices about what they would like their lives to be. Also, if they ever had a child, what they would want for that child – and how would they like that child to impact the world?

Communicating with them on an age-appropriate level that they could understand and relate to, the results were quite astounding. The children who had questionable motives eventually disappeared, because they felt they didn't measure up. The ones who stayed grabbed the gold ring – so to speak – and ran with it.

I remember one of Stephan's favorite friends. As an adult, he's become enormously successful. A talented artist, he designed my brochure for the meditation journey that I used during Stephan's upbringing. I remember the day he told me I'd had a positive influence in the success he's enjoying. Today, he's a world-class artist enjoying global distribution of his work.

The sweet irony is that he grew up with Stephan and witnessed my process *as it was being created!*

I was also careful about choosing Stephan's reading library. I placed carefully selected books on personal development in key places in the house. I felt they could positively impact his consciousness.

These sources contributed significantly to forming the foundation of my son's mental attitude.

Stephan's Story
Part 3

When Stephan was in his first year of high school, he was offered a one-year pilot program for gifted children. This was offered to students who appeared to seek innovative ways to deal with problem-solving. Stephan asked me what I thought and, after speaking with the teacher, I believed the program was resonant with what I hoped to accomplish for him. I was also delighted he was chosen as a student who wanted to pursue creativity and excellence.

I encouraged him and gave him the support to excel in the one-time project. He still fondly remembers his teacher, who today stands out to him as a beacon in his life and as a leader who helped him stretch his capacities.

A few years before that, I'd purchased Napolean Hill's legendary book, *Think and Grow Rich*, which I placed in my personal home library. I'd taken on a commitment to learn about success as a science and I used my commute to my job – involving six trains a day – to devour anything I could on the subject.

Why did certain people excel? What fired up some people to become all they could be; to utilize their potential to the fullest? I was learning that both achievement *and* prosperity can be attained with a value system intact, and that there was a spiritual component to attainment – *if* that attainment included giving back something to society in the form of a contribution.

It was at this time that I became very ill. Previous to that, I experienced a series of major traumas including the death of a brother *and* a sister, my mother's heart attack, a mugging I sustained at knife point, and the end of a long-standing relationship.

This series of "blows" to my mind and body resulted in a rapidly declining physiological state that included an enormous and rapid weight loss. The cumulative effects of the foundation I created for myself sustained me, carrying me through that terribly difficult time.

Stephan grew up very quickly during those two years of my ill health, not only from overcoming the worries of a concerned son, but also by becoming my caretaker. Interestingly, this was when he also learned about dietary supplements and made sure I took them daily.

Returning from school each day, Stephan was faced with the fear of the possible consequences of my drastic ill health, together with the intense motivation to save the one remaining parent in his life. The concern and fear in his eyes is something I'll never forget.

In this "crash-course," he learned the true meaning of caretaking, giving, loving, and concern.

During this precarious time, Stephan spent many nights in his bunk bed, reading a chapter daily of the *Laws of Success*, by Napolean Hill. His resolve to focus and rise above his circumstances and become successful burned as brightly within him as the aluminum clip-on light that shone on his book, imprinting a road map in the synapses of his brain.

The residue of that concern is very much alive today in Stephan's commitment to creating formulas that promote the health and well-being of numerous people across the country.

Everything that happened to Stephan during those challenging two years ultimately paved the way toward his future success.

Stephan's Story
Part 4

At some point in his early high school years, I intuitively felt the next step for Stephan was to experience selected role models in his life. I sensed this was going to play a critical and important part in the shaping of his identity. The lack of a father for him bore deeply in my heart and I vowed that his first role model should be a spiritual advisor, as that would create a foundation for his whole life. I later realized that role models can be part of every child's foundation in life.

It was shortly after this that I met the perfect individual for both Stephan and for myself.

Through a friend, I met a lady – let's call her a 'passing ship in the night' – who, after meeting me, determined that I should call someone named David – and she gave me his telephone number. These and other seemingly 'casual' occurrences became much more commonplace as I asked for guidance.

David represented many things; he was a successful actor, a coach, and a therapist. Most of all, however, he was deeply rooted into his own spirituality. The challenges he'd faced in his youth – being brought up without a father – and in his life generally, enabled him to access wisdom from a multitude of sources within himself: spiritually, psychologically, and practically.

Experiencing David's spiritual and psychological nurturing gave me an enormous sense of support. It was also a welcome adjunct in Stephan's life to have a father-type figure he looked up to and respected enormously.

David helped me to face my own pain and fears, mediated for my son and me when our wills clashed, and helped Stephan to get in touch with his spirituality and sensitivity. For a long time, David remained a strong presence in our lives.

Stephan's Story
Part 5

"Successful," to me, meant "doing what you wanted to do in your life and getting the desired result." Just as yin and yang are opposite ends of a balance, I wanted Stephan to become familiar with another role model who had integrated worldly success into his life while embodying humanistic/spiritual values into his accomplishments – someone who was a living example of this kind of success. Stephan was a good student in attracting mentors in many areas of life.

So far, we created an educational, spiritual, and – now – a role model that manifested prosperity in the outer world.

Again, the right person appeared through a casual acquaintance. His name was Joseph. He was the person I felt would be a good role model for Stephan, for worldly success – put into practice through the right values.

A meeting was arranged and I decided that my son was ready to learn from Joseph.

Joseph had built a large organization based on the success of a nutritional product. There were several meetings each week. I attended many of them with Stephan and I watched the glow in his eyes – reflecting the hunger to learn, the admiration and the respect for a leader who also combined spiritual growth with worldly success.

I also felt the germination within him of the desire to *achieve* on his own; to have a calling and to follow it with passion and resolve.

In time, Stephan was leading his own seminars based on the books he was reading and the role models that he both attracted and admired. He was hungry to learn and became Joseph's special prodigy as he promoted the product Joseph was connected with.

At fifteen years old, Stephan was grossing an income of almost $1000.00 per month! He was also learning ways to interact with different kinds of people and fully coming into his own.

Months after this, Stephan was faced with his first great disappointment: The company that manufactured the product decided to market it another way and bypassed the hardworking distributors who had brought it into the market through other users.

The news of the company filing chapter eleven and, thus, of the end of this opportunity altogether, came all too soon.

Behind a locked door, I heard my son audibly releasing his pent-up feelings of grief and shock. The tears I shed for him were mixed with gratitude for our sessions together, enabling him to expel these feelings of hurt from his mind, body, and spirit the right way.

Afterwards, when he was able to talk, I told Stephan failure was not falling down; failure was not getting up *after* you fall down. He resolved never again to work for another company but, instead, to become his own boss and make his own decisions.

Little did either of us know, but possibilities that neither of us had dreamed about were opening up for Stephan.

Stephan's Story
Part 6

Stephan had a good foundation now. On the academic level, he'd attended college for one and a half years. He felt he wasn't getting what he needed to apply to his life experience at that time, so he decided to leave college.

After my two-year stint with health challenges, I started to improve and was ready to resume working again. On my first job, my effective telemarketing skills were brought to the attention of the sales manager, who was extremely impressed.

Eventually, he persuaded me to consider the possibility of a future partnership, through one of my customers who trusted me. Because of that trust, I was able to acquire the venture capital to go into business, and started operating from my home in New York City. This was an excellent opportunity for Stephan – who was not yet in his 20's – to obtain the business and telephone skills *he needed for his* future ambitions. He also participated in the step-by-step construction of the business from the beginning.

Before my business expanded, he decided – prematurely – to venture out on his own, seeking his own office space. He worked hard and long with partners who didn't 'stick,' and had his first experience with 'hard work' that didn't contain the factor of 'know-how.'

In the meantime, my business had grown from a room in my apartment to three branches – the main one being in the world-famous Empire State Building. I invited Stephan back to join us in our new offices, so he could continue learning.

As the son of the owner of the business, Stephan started showing signs of arrogance, because he felt that he was 'privileged.' I felt it was time to emphasize humility with regard to what it takes to create something of value. He had to get another job, which involved getting up at 4:00 a.m. every morning to mix the dough in a cookie franchise chain.

Within two weeks, he learned the value of time, money, and effort. I still remember his comment, at the end of that job: "Mom – I *got* it!"

This was indeed a time for some stringent life lessons for Stephan. I acknowledge his strength and warrior-like spirit, and am grateful that these lessons were learned at an early age when disillusionment didn't have a chance to set in.

Stephan's Story
Part 7

The year was 1985. It was Stephan's 18th birthday! It was time to get a very special gift for him – something that would stay with him for the rest of his life.

It was time for his *ultimate* role model!

Anthony Robbins had achieved enormous success by doing what he loved, and became a man of great wealth. This is a combination that has always fascinated me. I had learned, from his example, that you *can* achieve prosperity living through your values. When I heard that Tony was conducting a seminar, called *Financial Destiny,* in Del Mar, California, I knew this was the perfect birthday gift I was looking for; a value-driven role model who acquired both achievement and meaning in his life.

Anthony Robbins lived in a beautiful castle, and it was there that my son and I stayed for four days as participants in his workshop/seminar.

The experience was a very powerful and concentrated course in both defining and setting up specific goals to realize your dreams. The energy in the room with the other participants was very charged and stimulating, and we all stretched our "muscles" to put down on paper what we wanted to achieve and create in our lives.

The impact on Stephan was startling. He now had a clear road map to the realization of his life dreams, and the support to stay motivated. We all noticed Tony's extraordinary energy level and – when break time came around – Stephan noticed that the food being served was all vegetarian.

From that day on – for two years – he became a strict vegetarian, taking control of his own well-being. Stephan later discovered that his O Blood type needed healthy meat so, though he still maintained his health goals, he added that necessary component. I gave him an 'A' for wanting to be like Tony Robbins, who represented both discipline and excellence.

To this day, Stephan gives priority to his health and well-being with consistency and discipline.

Stephan clearly wanted to create his own business; something that he alone started and would be accountable to and for. While involved in my business, he met one of my managers who subsequently became his first partner. I gave them the seed money to get started.

He tried many different venues; none of them really worked. During this time, Stephan was also attending night school, so he could get his college degree. One day, I urged him to attend a seminar about successfully marketing an effective weight-loss product. It took about five different invitations from me to finally get him to the meeting. When he returned from the seminar, Stephan told me he'd decided this was the way he wanted to go: marketing a weight-loss product in a *then* 30 billion dollar annual industry. That figure is much higher today.

"Why reinvent the wheel, Mom?"

Things began to change very rapidly at that point. Stephan took the initiative to find a manufacturer and, after naming his new product, I helped him open up a merchant credit line so he could accept credit card payments.

He subsequently branched out into various health-enhancing products, and his business grew from that point on.

Stephan's Story
Part 8

Within all of us at birth is a hidden treasure. With parenting, we have a sacred charge to gently coax that gift into fullness. There's a story about the monarch butterfly that is a wonderful lesson about growing into fullness. A little boy thought by helping the caterpillar grow faster, he would manually accelerate the process. When the time came for the butterfly to be in fullness, it couldn't fly. It had been crippled because it didn't receive what it needed to be whole. Therefore, we could never savor its multicolored beauty and flight. Its gift remained unspoken.

What can your child become? How many lives might he or she impact? And what is the singular beauty inside him or her that the world could celebrate?

Your child may be eager to become a doctor, counselor, ballerina, or a street sweeper. Every child has a different calling. Martin Luther King, Jr. said, "If a man is called to be a street sweeper, he should sweep streets even as Michelangelo painted, or Beethoven composed music, or Shakespeare wrote poetry. He should sweep streets so well that all the hosts of heaven and earth will pause to say, 'here lived a great street sweeper who did his job well.'"

Stephan wanted the liberty of free enterprise – to create and prosper while also helping other people improve their lives. That was his goal. His focus and perseverance brought him there.

As a result of the guidance he received during his upbringing, he achieved his dreams – well beyond the fullness he envisioned. Imagine the possibilities for your children!

Stephan was now in his own business – working at home and beginning to see indications of a viable and profitable enterprise. He'd just graduated with honors from college and, during a social night out, met his future wife, Lori.

As a marketing executive with Revlon, Lori experienced the breadth and scope of the corporate infrastructure, while Stephan had the vision and creativity of an entrepreneur.

In many ways, it was a perfect match.

Those early days of working in a small room in my New York apartment enabled Stephan to learn computer skills. He'd experienced a negative association with a former 'partner' who was very computer literate. During the time they worked together, this partner used those advanced skills not only as leverage to prolong his partnership with Stephan, but also as a tool to make some deliberate mistakes that hurt the business in some serious ways.

It had taken a while for Stephan to correct those problems but, after the corrections were made, Stephan was on his way – with many learned lessons under his belt.

In 1996, after a vacation in Florida, Lori and Stephan decided to move down to Destin and take the business there. After they were married, in February, 1997, their apartment served as their first effort to expand the business. In less than one and a half years, they rented a corporate space in Niceville that housed about 50 employees.

These days, Great American Products is enjoying extraordinary growth, and operates from a 10,000 square foot building owned by the company, all under the guiding hands of my son and his wife.

Stephan is now heard on the radio all over the country, and his infomercials are seen by many. His college has awarded him honorary recognition for his achievements – both in print and by creating a video of Stephan as an exemplification and role model of extraordinary success.

It's been an incredible journey from that day on the service elevator when I vowed to guide and mentor my son to pursue excellence, and inculcate success skills in him that would make all of this a reality. I never dreamed, however, that his success would be so vast.

It's my hope you will pass the torch – this new legacy – to your children. That, my dear reader, is my definition of True Wealth!

I'm here to tell you that you *can* master your life and become a wonderful example for the child you're raising.

Your first step is to understand that, if you want something different and desire more than you have now, all you have to do is be willing to do something different to get it. The shift you make will give you personal power and the resulting confidence to transform your life in front of your eyes.

Yes – *you*.

You can change your present circumstances by using the same process that helped me turn my life around. You have all you need and I'm honored to be your guide.

Here's the <u>*best*</u> news: you don't even need to have my initials!

In the rest of this book, you'll find the 7 **Keys** that can turn *your* life around!

Part 3

Your New Blueprint for Raising Extraordinary Kids: The 7 Keys for Parenting in the 21st Century – A New Paradigm

• Key #1: If You Want Something You Never Had, You Have To Do Something You Never Did

I'd like to begin this first **Key** by giving you some background on how I developed the process you'll be learning.

The year was 1982. We were in the midst of a big recession and the President of the United States had declared a war on drugs. I was a divorced welfare mom living in New York City on West 73rd Street near Lincoln Center. Back in '82, West 73rd was infested with drug dealers and prostitutes.

As a concerned parent, I sat down with my son one day and asked if he was smoking pot. I knew many of his friends had access to marijuana. My son looked at me and said, "You know, mom, I tried it, but I get higher on life!"

I was overwhelmed with gratitude for my son – not only because he was able to speak his truth, but that he felt comfortable talking to me about it. That's what this book is about. It's about your son or daughter and what needs to happen *first*, in order to shape their values and become the best they can be. Then, and only then, can they make empowering choices *regardless of outside negative influences.*

They'll be able to speak and live in their individual truth and hold strong against the tide of negative peer pressure, TV celebrities who are dysfunctional, overwhelming societal changes – all kinds of negativity. Rather than curing the damaging results of outside negative influences, this book is about the preemptive measures that will bring results in creating your child's true destiny.

We're talking about a new paradigm, which is a fundamental shift or change in a belief system. How does this relate to being a parent? It's natural and understandable to be focused on the thought, "What do I do or say to my child, to prevent or correct attitudes that I don't want and create behavior and attitudes that I do want?" The paradigm you'll learn about, and that has the scientific validation mentioned previously, is one which starts with making you – the parent – gain a greater degree of personal effectiveness. This will *naturally* give you access to innovative ways of dealing with problems and accessing creative solutions.

Again, according to Einstein, it's only by thinking differently that we get different results. When we experience a paradigm shift, we see everything from a different perspective. An additional shift or change comes when our subsequent actions are different and we function differently as a result of that new perspective. We can't always change the world around us. Life happens, but we *can* change the way we see it and what we do about it. You can change your present circumstances by using the same process that helped me turn my life around.

• Key #2: Getting Centered, Staying Centered: Creating New Habits for Better Results

I want to tell you about a dream I had. It will give you a picture of what was happening to me at the lowest time of my life.

I dreamed I was suspended on a trapeze swing in the middle of nowhere. While I was hanging there, I noticed a swing swaying back and forth seductively, almost within arm's reach. I thought, if I could grab it, it would open up something new and promising for me. Simply put, it would change my life. But, I had to wait for the right moment – precisely when the two swings met – to dare make the leap.

It felt like an eternity. At the precise moment, I leapt off the old swing, grabbed the new one and felt the terrifying excitement of trusting myself enough to decide to make a life change.

And that's exactly what I did.

Even under the best of circumstances, when opportunity comes, we're all faced with choices, just like in my dream – to grab the swing or not; to stay stuck or not.

But, what would it take to trust ourselves enough to make the life changes we need and want to make? Also, what do we have to do to let that trust propel us to move forward, motivated by a strong sense of conviction?

I believe I've found an answer. As you practice these principles, it will give you the secret of easily accessing, developing and strengthening the trust that lies within your own inner resources, just as I did. This leads to an inner motivation that doesn't need 'pumping up.' *Change* then shows up naturally.

We all face challenges. In today's world, they're compounded by the insecurity of the economy and our planet in crisis, along with the pressures of daily life, including measuring up as a possible mate, parent, daughter/son-in-law, or employee, for example. The digital age, in addition, has brought both an accelerated pace of life and unnatural aspects to our relationships.

Remember the mother and child I spoke about, who were having a lunch where both mother and child were looking at their smart phones throughout their entire meal? Not *once* did they engage with one another.

These elements can bring about feelings of isolation and confusion and cause a sense of frustration. This can lead to feelings of disconnection and, eventually, to depression.

We all have a lot on our plates. This affects every aspect of our daily lives. But know this: how we live our daily lives becomes a central factor that influences our children and the way they see us. If we let our lives be filled with negative thoughts and emotions, we shouldn't be surprised to find our children doing the same. When we allow our lives to be filled with positive thoughts and emotions, we can be pleasantly surprised to find our children following suit, because they naturally reflect our actions and decisions.

When we as parents manage our stress well and develop good relationship skills, our children will mimic this behavior. One very effective accelerator of progress in handling stress and relationships – which, of course, impacts every area of our lives, in addition to our parenting – is to draw upon new ways of changing our thought patterns and awareness or going to another level and seeing "newly."

I knew my current life wasn't working and I didn't want to kid myself into believing that my old ways of thinking would change my life. Many of us live our lives accepting old habits and conditions that no longer work; we fall into a daily rut. We're comfortable with what we know. What I wanted was a shift that could give me a mindset that could filter into my daily life – not just to have the ability to overcome the ups and downs, but also to enjoy my daily life. What a concept!

At the point when I began questioning what I needed to do to create new habits, I experienced one of my greatest shifts. I had that dream where I was grabbing a new swing and I realized then that, yes! I *could* change.

But I had to find a way to automatically shift my beliefs into a new framework, a new grid from which positive potential would be a natural outcome for my child and for me. I needed a new set of critical life skills that would bring a different perspective and a different result.

It wasn't about any form of psychotherapy or fixing my childhood issues. It was about deep fundamental change – the paradigm shift we talked about in **Key #1**. It's about becoming a role model for our children and for ourselves. It's about *being*, and taking a stand for the best within us, allowing our God-given gifts to manifest themselves in the world as a result.

It's about bringing forth and nourishing that God-given seed of potential that lies in every single child.

There wasn't anything like this out there, so I knew I had to create it.

Hands down, this book will give you the tools to naturally bring about the changes you want to see in your life.

This is what **Key #2** is all about. It's about *making the shift* so that you can experience change.

Believe me, I wasn't quite sure how or when the shift would happen, but I knew I *had* to trust myself. I had nowhere else to go and couldn't, on a deeper level, believe I was put on this Earth to struggle without end. Some of us feel this same way at times.

In short, I knew I *had* to change my thinking. When I realized that the power to change was in me and I was led to *learn* to access that power, I knew the transformations I was about to make would affect the life of my child, too – a life I was about to shape, regardless of what was going on in the world or with me.

I was the guardian of my child's life! How did I want him to turn out? Did I want him to be taken advantage of as a vulnerable victim in the world, or to have the powerful armor of a developed inner wisdom handed down from a wise parent-mentor? I dreamed my child would grow up to become successful, an upstanding member of his community. I also wanted his children to be beneficiaries of the lessons he learned about locating, developing, and living through your values.

All of this emerged from my own self-development, and from a passion to create new habits that would bring different results.

To get there, I had to let go of the old swing and grab the new one.

It's my goal that my experiences will teach you to do the same and to create new habits that bring out life-changing results for you.

We most likely all realize we can't isolate our children from the world around them, nor deny what's going on. Still, we can certainly prepare ourselves to give them the tools they need to become the best they can be.

It was at this point that I realized I didn't have to learn *parenting* skills. I had to learn *self-fulfillment* skills. The truth is: the parent has to change his or her perspective. Then, the child will *reflect* that new, different perspective – and the resulting positive behavior that comes out of this new perspective.

So – if it all begins with us, how do we make the changes and have them feel natural, a part of us?

I found that I had to elevate my thinking to a new level, to overcome obstacles and move in the direction of my ideal life easily and naturally – as both a person and as a parent.

I had to wonder: Is this new and expanded awareness something others refer to as "higher consciousness" – seeing new possibilities by uplifting our thinking, seeing new vistas and solutions? I started to understand that attracting and manifesting – or bringing into reality – what you want in your life emerges from a new perspective arising from an uplifted consciousness. If we want new solutions for a better life, indeed we *must* nourish our thoughts and feelings by uplifting them or raising them to what some people call a higher perspective, or "a higher consciousness."

The status quo will change *nothing* except to invite negative gravity to lower our consciousness and have us live beneath our God-given gifts and possibilities.

Science now has the evidence proving the effectiveness of going within, using meditation or centering in the areas of health, sports, psychology, and general well-being, to improve one's performance or results. Many major medical schools offer Continuing Medical Education on the healing power of body-mind practices today, including meditation. Recent studies (Harvard Medical School) also suggest the anti-aging benefits of meditation.

In **Key #1**, I discussed going "inside" and I talked about how *asking* gave me answers. The exact answers will be different for all of us. What will remain a constant is that you'll experience a shift in your life as a result of the answers you've discovered within yourself after following the process.

It was during the first stages of going inside myself and looking for answers to my life that I gained an understanding of the rich reward of what some refer to as "centering," or "grounding."

I like to call this process centering or grounding, too. It seems to fit how I feel afterwards.

Science has found that, when you're centered, it actually changes your brain waves, balancing the left and right hemispheres of the brain and allowing you to use whole-brain consciousness. When you use *whole* brain consciousness, you experience an expanded capacity for creative solutions, answers to challenges come more easily, your capabilities increase, and your reasoning becomes more sound.

You're able, from this place, to discover solutions not available to you before, to solve problems more effectively and to see the old habits fall away naturally. The new habits you develop will serve you more effectively in the 21st century, with all the challenges it presents. You'll discover that the limitless possibilities provided to you from this place are timeless, *regardless* of outside events.

The Einstein dictum actually comes to fruition as your perspective begins to operate on an entirely new level.

In order to access this level that opened up expanded possibilities, I had to enter a new place and set a different platform for the different outcomes I wanted. A simple centering or grounding technique was what I used.

I found a comfortable physical position in which to sit and a way that could simply help me to connect to the quiet place inside me. You may have a different name for it other than "centering" but, as long as you learn to practice this process, it doesn't matter what you call it. In the end, what matters most to your child is how you show up, handling the challenges and stressors of daily life.

Centering helps you attain the right perspective to do this. It's imperative for us as parents to stay centered and connected. Then, you can easily create the context for an exciting new way to experience your time as a parent, being close to your child and giving him or her a chance to live life to its fullest potential in ways that are satisfying for both of you.

In this quiet place that I call centering, you'll develop a sense of safety beyond worldly and personal fear – a place where, by turning inward, your thinking becomes clear.

Turning inward helped me do that. It also helped me discover guidelines for decision making; it was the beginning of my ability to change my old habits. When I began this practice every day, I noticed that, when I approached my son to care for or to relate to him, I felt calmer, more at peace and able to be more *present* for him. I didn't bring my "stuff" with me. It felt like "clean" parenting.

In addition to expressing my love for him more easily, I experienced fewer fears than had previously monopolized my thoughts.

There's no need to make this process of centering difficult or to separate it from other habits in our lives. When we're hungry, we eat. When we want clean teeth, we brush them. If we need sleep, we rest. If we want a better life, small daily steps on a consistent basis will get us there.

It's really that simple.

With the hectic pace of life today, simplicity is important. You can integrate centering into your life, making it as easy as brushing your teeth or going to sleep. Look at it as just another part of your daily routine!

But first, before we get to the actual act of centering, there is an additional important step – one that distinguishes this process from others!

BEFORE CENTERING:

I have found that, before I "fill the cup" of my consciousness with centering, it's important to first release any feelings of negativity or hurt – or simply to express the chattering of the 'monkey mind' – and get it out of the way. I've found that, for me, journaling is the way to do this.

Releasing those feelings in your journal will prepare you to access and to *refill* your consciousness with a clean slate – with purity and authenticity from your deeper self. If you were an artist, you'd want to paint something new on a clean canvas. I see every day as a new painting – a new way, new choices, new colors – to create the kind of day I want to live.

Buy a new journal. Date each day and use it to release your innermost feelings. Take your time. Remember – journaling records what you feel and experience emotionally and mentally, whereas keeping a diary is often simply making a record of events and happenings. When I journal, I listen to beautiful, non-vocal music.

Begin your journaling by releasing and emptying any feelings of hurt, pain, concerns, etc. When you do this, you bring Clean Parenting to the "plate," because your child gets the best of You.

Now, you're ready for centering.

The Centering Process

Centering – or grounding – is a means of getting into a place where change *can* happen. An example of this is what's been termed the "zone" in physical fitness. It's the place where you know physical fitness magic happens; the work you did getting there enabled you to realize a feeling of power, momentum, and the kind of extraordinary results that you earned...*because* you put the effort into it. Achievement in physical fitness feels great! Centering leads you to explore new regions of your mind and spirit where you become "fit" and find your best self. There's also no better feeling than one of self-achievement in that area.

To get centered, fit with your mind and spirit:

Physics tells us that nature hates a vacuum. A new, clean space has been created. Now you're ready to fill that space with centering, which will give you access to your best self.

Find a quiet place and allow yourself to become totally relaxed in this new, open, clean space. Breathe naturally. Pay attention to your breath. Focus on it and stay with it, so distractions won't take hold. When you've reached a calm center point, stay and revel in it.

You'll know when you're there. Some people use a timer that has a soft sound, to signal the end of their daily centering – others simply bask in it; whatever works. Start slowly, doing only about five minutes or so in the beginning. There's no need to force it; you'll eventually expand the process to a longer duration. The important thing is that a shift takes place from how you felt the moment before you centered, and how you feel during and after the centering. You should experience a calm feeling of well-being; a sense of mental "order."

The secret is to do a centering process each morning before the activity or schedule of your daily life seeps in. Make it a priority *before* turning on the radio, TV, or answering email. The important thing is to begin the day with centering before *anything else* occupies your mind.

If this is like something you've already been doing, that's great. What's important is *daily consistency* and making it a priority at the *beginning* of your day *every* day.

You may wonder, "Am I doing it right? Is this working yet?"

Yes, you are and, yes, it is. Notice the small changes at first and observe what feels different. Soon, you'll notice *measurable* results.

Remember: we didn't "dive" into our centering; we cleared our consciousness first by journaling out our feelings – whatever they may be.

This is when we can then refill our "cup" – consciousness – from a new, "clean," higher place.

After the initial newness of centering, this time that you spend with yourself will become comfortable and comforting – a place of peace, your home. This new home will come to feel very inviting. When you've felt a kind of completeness, not unlike being satisfied after a full meal, count slowly backwards, from ten to one, to return back to the present moment.

Remember: You feed your body. Now, you'll learn to feed your *soul* – with a different kind of food: *Spiritual* nutrition.

Soon, you'll experience both an expansion and enhancement of your ordinary capacities. This gives you, the parent, an opportunity to have the day filtered through the centering experience, rather than you being at the mercy of what the day imposes on you.

I hope it's becoming clear this isn't about what you say or do to or with your child, but what you do as the *parent* and, as a natural consequence, what that does to the child-parent relationship.

Here's what happens in this process of getting accustomed to centering: you're making room and space for access to other areas of your mind, heart, and soul; you become quiet and undistracted. Through consistent and regular practice, this will be your private space, your calm safe harbor that will bring guidance for your life and turn your questions into answers.

In terms of my experience with centering and its effect on my son, I felt I was nourishing myself and, at the same time, as if I was feeding breast milk to my child, knowing there was no one else in the world but me who could duplicate that food. It brought us closer because what I was offering him was the best of myself.

What better way can you choose to "nourish" your child than to offer the very best of his own parent or guardian?

Remember, it's easy: all you're doing is starting a new habit – making a simple, enjoyable addition to your routine that will become a daily practice you can integrate easily into your day. The life-changing results will be more than worth the minimal effort it requires.

You may want to set your alarm for a time to wake up, so your morning routine can include your practice of both a journaling and a centering process. By engaging in this process every morning, you're able to more easily and readily relax and let go, setting the foundation for your day and living the way you want to – easily, smoothly, experiencing a steady, cumulative empowerment that's more than just an occasional good feeling.

Wouldn't it feel *great* to have more control over your life? Think what that will do for you and for your relationship with your child. It's truly there for the taking – by simply reaping the full benefits of accessing your own wisdom!

The influence of this centering technique on every aspect of your life continues even after your children have grown and are reaping their own rewards from it. Now that my son is an adult and parent, I still regularly do the centering process.

This practice helped me rise out of poverty and become the CEO of my own million dollar company.

If I created the life that I wanted, starting from where I did, so can you. That's why I'm sharing this legacy with you. I paved the way, so take this shortcut to your own wisdom and better parenting and *grab that swing!*

There's more to come!

• Key #3: Aligning with What Really Matters To You – Living In Your Values Zone

It's undeniable. We're involved in the lives of our children every day and they're watching us. What are we teaching them on a daily basis? What example are we instilling in them? Are we positive role models? If not, what can we do to change, so we're the role models we'd most want our children to follow?

With all this and more as a backdrop, how do we grab that swing and make the shift – in the midst of doing dishes, shopping for groceries, meal planning, and doing our best to keep the love alive?

Here's what's true:

Changing your life cannot be accomplished by putting on a veneer, wearing a happy face, or by adopting a "fake-it-until-you-make-it" attitude. What must be changed, however, is our consciousness itself. What follows automatically is the reality of who we then really are.

Our children will "get" this change, even nonverbally.

As mentioned before, in the realm of physical fitness, you feel an exhilaration that comes from your persistent efforts, from your practice and – yes – from your resulting achievement. Now *hold that thought!* What if you could have a psychological *and* emotional experience that gave you the *same* kind of exhilaration as that physical effort and achievement?

Being centered and focused is a process that brings you to that space by consistent adherence to the process itself.

You begin from where you are and, eventually, build what we might call those "centering" muscles that bring you to a new level of awareness, giving you a greater understanding about what your purpose is and who you are in the world.

Sure, what you think and feel – and the thoughts you carry all day long – are in a different zone from the physical one. Even though you can't see them, however, feelings and thoughts show up in your life in many different ways, including discontent, sadness, or feeling you're not living the life you want. Nonetheless, you make choices about life based on your thoughts and feelings.

What kind of choices do *you* want to make?

The **Keys** I've detailed in this book are about raising the bar and making new choices – without struggle, but with the same kind of effort you might expend with *any* goal you want to attain.

It *doesn't* simply take you there without regular participation on your part, but the mere participation itself is a major part of what makes the achievement of your goals possible.

This is about tapping the silent zone of your inner life – your thoughts and feelings. You don't hear any noise from walking or from being on a treadmill. There aren't any groans from doing crunches. However, when you tap into this place through centering, you get into what I call the "Values Zone" – the inner awareness equivalent of the "zone" that's proven to carry top athletes, artists, and musicians beyond the extraordinary in performance and achievement throughout their lives.

In this place, with consistency and with your resolve for a better life experience for you and for your children, you'll come into contact with your true values: what's truly important to you, never to be compromised.

What will that mean to you?

1. A strong motivation to achieve the results you want.
2. Rewards beyond your expectations.

This method of finding your core beliefs in the Values Zone will bring out the answers that mean the most to you – whether they relate to your dilemmas, to your pain, your discontent, and eventually to your joy. It will reveal to you exactly what you need to do to turn your life around in a practical, natural, and consistent way. This new direction will be in perfect harmony with what you hold dear – your true value system for you and for your child.

Your expanding awareness then becomes a vessel of light and you bring this light to others. Your child will sense naturally that you're someone to listen to, a guide or mentor they *want* to follow.

Your child will begin to trust you more as well. In the realm of your new growing awareness, things will automatically fall into place because you now have a framework to reference as you move toward the manifestation of those values that are related to both of you. This is when your children will *see* what you value and what's important to you. They'll choose to adapt those values for their own and, by extension, this will help them to birth more of their own values.

The values you incorporate into your daily life are the values your child will see on a daily basis. You will examine and question more closely the ways in which you make decisions. Your doubts will begin to disappear and you'll replace them with the assurance of trusting yourself about how you live your life. You *and* your children will get these results when you become aligned with your Values Zone.

Until now, there hasn't been a blueprint for doing this and you've done the best you know how without a solid foundation to guide you. But, now there *is* a way and you're holding it in your hands. You don't have to grope and put out fires any more. Those wonderful self-help and spiritual books that I read – and I've read a *lot* of them – all contained universal values that we hold dear and, as such, that formed the framework for me to create this system.

The next step was to take everything I learned and find a way to share it in a practical way, because the context of discovering something original in the first place can be very different from the context of presenting it to others. That's exactly what I've done. I figured out how to help other parents to understand the process, regardless of their background.

Now you can explore and open up the unused muscles of your thoughts, ideas, and feelings that make up your inner life, then flex them and find your deepest potential and gifts – just as I did. That's what this book is about. That's why I wrote this book for you.

What will you find as a result of this process?

- A growing confidence in your ability to make the right decisions; decisions not only for your life but also in relation to your child's needs.

- Actions will begin to parallel what's important to you and to your child.
- People who resonate with your own ideals.
- Your true values – maintaining a healthy environment for your child.
- An innate sense of organization and order.
- Improved relationships with your significant other and with the people around you.
- Limitless opportunities, making life feel like a candy store.
- An ongoing sense of being restored on a daily basis.

Who could have known that I would go from being on welfare to creating a process that enabled me to raise an extraordinary child while becoming a business owner of a million dollar company myself?

And I only possessed the skills of a poet and musician!

I believe that, when you get in touch with the treasure that lies beneath the surface, you hit "pay dirt." You've then developed the ability to become a better person, a more loving parent – and you've cultivated the ability to create the life you want.

The best part is, once you open yourself to changing the way you look at things, you'll begin to experience fundamental, lasting change in the way you want your life to be. Not just an insight here or a workshop there, but deep, fundamental *lasting* change.

Imagine what that can mean to you!

Do you think this is the kind of person and parent who could raise an extraordinary child? You bet it is!

I did it. So can you.

Now you're ready for **Key #4** – an exciting step. You're ready to become a *mentor*.

• Key #4: Easing Into Mentorship – Parenting for the 21st Century

One day, when my son was about six years old, he was helping me put dishes in the dishwasher. There was a particularly beautiful glass goblet someone had given me and I kept it aside.

He said, "Mommy, why don't you put that in, too?"

I answered, "I don't want it to break, because I won't be able to get another one."

He said, "Don't worry, it'll be okay."

I hesitatingly put it in with the other articles.

When the cycle was done, I pulled out the top drawer of the dishwasher, and my son put his hand into it, to lift the goblet. As he did so, it fell apart in pieces. He looked at me, wide-eyed with fear and about to cry, his little shoulders hunched in, arms folded over his chest.

I saw the terror in his face and was acutely aware that my reaction, at that precise moment, would be instrumental in shaping my son's life. What memory of this event did I want him to have?

Immediately, my mind went through a quick calculation of possible choices. I instantly decided that, rather than punishing him because he'd given me the wrong advice, I'd rather have a broken glass than possibly break my young son's spirit.

I softened, looked at him, and asked, "Did you hurt yourself?" His little body relaxed and he came over to me to hug and thank me.

I won't ever forget that moment.

Looking back, the compassion and understanding that I was able to show him was a direct result of the effort that I'd been making to give my child the best of me – through this process.

Later on, the way I communicated with him and provided him with core skills for daily living ultimately became the foundation for his extraordinary success at such a young age. My son became a multi-millionaire before the age of 30!

To this day, his trust in me is unshakable and he's replicated this work with his own children.

In Rollo May's book, *"The Courage to Create,"* which I also picked up at the "right" time, it was emphasized that we all have the need to perpetuate something; to leave something lasting. It's a natural urge. This book will empower you to discover, give, and leave your very best self to your children, and a legacy to pass down to their children.

The virtues of good parenting cannot be overstated. As a biologically instinctive process, healthy parenting fosters mutual love and nurturing. We as parents know this and we've felt it, but the parent-as-mentor role is far less familiar to most of us. It's a new concept that takes you a step further. Mentoring means you've stepped up to the plate; you're expanding your abilities, compassion, understanding, and empathy.

Your parenting method, now blending with mentoring, helps you begin to replace punitive methods with communication, empathy, compassion, and guidance.

This is not about child psychology; it's about *parental self-development and fulfillment*. When you develop yourself and feel fulfilled, you're able to almost effortlessly pass that feeling on to your child.

Mentoring is also a conscious decision, with specific proactive steps, to guide the child and adult within a safe, psychological environment, to tap into the child's potential and to find their passion and life's meaning.

Of course, there are times when children have to learn lessons. Once, my son was asked not to use the vacuum because, if he did, he'd get a "Time Out," since he'd broken it once before.

He turned on the vacuum. It broke again and – sure enough – he got another "Time Out."

He never did it again. We must not confuse this loving inculcation of discipline with the harsh, punitive methods that some parents use unthinkingly. In this work, you'll learn effective ways of dealing with your child that will reduce the need for "discipline."

When a child learns an important lesson through example, by "teachable moments," it sets the stage for becoming a well-functioning adult.

We may have seen or heard about an extraordinary parent and his or her relationship with their child, but a new standard for consistent and dependable results is what's needed today, to shape our children's future.

I'd define a parental mentor this way:

> *One who is willing to make the necessary changes within themselves in order to provide extraordinary support, guidance, friendship, and respect to a child, with the aim of helping him or her to become a happy, healthy, fulfilled adult.*

Why is this so important now?

Based on the challenges of living today and what's happening in the world and to our children, there's an enormous need for a specific new key element in the everyday parenting process. This is what I call the blending of mentoring with parenting. Old forms of parenting will leave us in the dust, because they no longer meet the challenges of our time.

Again, look at the state of the world now and you'll see what's happening – that is, if you haven't already been personally affected by it. We see it every time we click on our TV or pick up a newspaper. It's saying, loud and clear:

The old ways of parenting are not enough and must be dramatically changed.

We have to decide: Do we want to put the effort into prevention, or into the cure – *after* the damage has been done?

It no longer works to think, "In my day, we did such and such while raising our children." Those days have passed. The world has changed and we need to rise to the occasion, to meet its challenges. It's a new day and, with it, we're creating a new way to help our children become all they can be and contribute their gifts to make the world a better place for everyone.

Mentoring by parents or grandparents or other close caretakers enables us to keep up with the challenges of the times by raising the bar for our children, so they can meet and master those challenges.

We've now arrived at the bountiful table of mentoring. First, we'll define traditional mentoring, then we'll look at a new model of the 21st century: the parent mentor.

What exactly *is* mentoring?

Roget's thesaurus lists the following terms for mentor: "advisor, coach, counselor, guide, guru, instructor, teacher, trainer, and tutor." Mentoring is one of the oldest and best forms of influence in the world. In fact, the word "mentor" comes from Greek mythology.

In today's business world, it describes a professional relationship in which an older, more experienced person lends a hand to a newcomer – often giving them a boost up the career ladder.

While a child today can receive valuable mentoring from such outside sources as teachers, scouting, or religious youth group leaders, the fact remains that home is where the parents are and that relationship far exceeds the child's limited contact with other sources. The parental relationship that includes nurturing and guidance will ultimately define your children, bring out their potential, and encourage them to aid in the healing and renewing of our society.

So – how does one become a mentor?

In light of breakthrough research described previously, parental self-development is, hands down, **The *Main* Key**. To develop the qualities to become a mentor, we've so far shown the following steps as the groundwork for this new paradigm:

> **Key #1** – Deciding we want a different experience than that which we presently have. We want *change*.
>
> **Key #2** – Creating a new habit of connecting with our personal source and activating it on a consistent, regular basis – an automatic habit much like brushing our teeth.
>
> **Key #3** – Having done **Key #2**, we then *automatically* begin tapping into our true values; being able to see what's *really* important and cannot be compromised. When you've accessed these values and live by them, your actions will reflect it and your child will naturally *get* it.

It's really as simple as that.

What, then, begins to happen?

As a result of consistently accessing the muscles that hold the wisdom of our core values, rather than the intellect and education of child psychology alone, we'll achieve a kind of "internal" fitness. With physical fitness, we achieve physical strength and power. With "internal" fitness, we begin to truly live our values and they're reflected in the outer world by the things, people, and circumstances that we manifest.

We're beginning to see – as a result of this consistency – a change in consciousness, in awareness. It's not so very different from getting results from consistent physical fitness – right?

Spending time centering is a priority for creating the platform of the day as *you* want it to be; it keeps you from living in a constant state of reaction to the day's happenings. It's also the place to get answers.

Here's what begins to happen: You'll naturally feel lighter, less anxious, and experience a sense of balance in your life with a feeling of ease. You'll be in a different place, a different state of mind. You'll feel restored and renewed on a daily basis. You'll find yourself on a smooth track, living preventively – not reactively.

You now have a new way and perspective for taking action that comes automatically and with ease; life feels more stress-free. You'll find people responding to you differently – to the positive changes that are now being seen on the "outside" as a result of the "inside" work you've done.

I remember when I started centering, people would ask me, "What are you doing differently? You seem calmer and happier!"

Well – I was! I'd shifted from being a stressed out mom to a caring, loving person involved in the everyday process of seeing and experiencing new insights, new feelings, new possibilities, new hope. I was on an exciting adventure with the days unfolding in new ways. I was beginning to experience a journey of growing self-fulfillment, and I brought that same energetic field to my parenting. Within the framework of my values, I had a blueprint for my days. I was beginning to flourish and the world was becoming my oyster.

That was also the time when I was urged to share my work.

You may recall my experience in the elevator while pregnant, having labor pains while being surrounded by garbage collected from each floor by the janitor. It was at that moment that I made my vow to not only change *my* life, but to both create *and* transfer a new legacy to my child. I had no idea how it was going to happen, but I knew I wanted to do it more than anything.

I kept that vow, and now I'm bringing that promise of a better life to you.

Now – let's talk about becoming a mentor. What does a parent do to become a mentor?

As a result of the steps you've been taking in the earlier **Keys**, almost like stepping up a ladder to reach a higher level, you'll have developed new abilities and capacities that will interface with your child's gifts and personality. You'll be led to say, speak, and act with the right response at the right time. That's different than relying on such lame statements as, "Listen to me or else," or "Because I'm the parent – that's why."

These responses create an adversarial relationship, causing disconnection. Then the child's goal is to avoid punishment, instead of seeking approval as a reward. We know what can happen afterward: looking for good feelings can turn into looking for approval in the wrong places.

Here are some of the ingredients of mentoring:

- Connecting and renewing your mind, heart and soul on a daily basis to become a better you. I like to think of it as a lamp that needs to be plugged in and turned on or you won't be able to read that book. So – plug in and you'll see the light!

- Creating a safe space and time with your child to foster trust, and to assure your child of your commitment to his or her growth.
- Discovering, supporting and nurturing the child's unique natural talents.
- Respecting the child's budding identity.
- Providing the child with a structure.

Just remember to do your daily centering magic and the rest will come naturally. It sounds too easy and that's what gets in the way most often. Trust your instincts – as long as they emerge from your daily connection.

Now you can see that mentoring isn't something you just do *for* your child. It's something you do for yourself and *with* your child. A mentor becomes someone a child can bounce ideas off of in the same way a player bounces ideas off a coach.

Probably the closest counterpart to a parental mentor is a good sports coach. Ideally, a coach does his best to build gently on a player's own strengths and lessen his weaknesses. The best coach offers guidance, then stands back and watches the action without condemnation. Even as he gives advice, he understands that it's the player who must perform. Ideally, the coach earns the trust of the player in the same way a parent can earn the trust of a child.

How does the coach do that? He builds confidence so the player can play and *win*.

That's exactly what you want for your child. You want your child to win! That's why the first three **Keys** are so important. That's where you begin to shift your energy, which will lead you to manifest the new results you desire.

Remember: New actions from a new place produce new results.

How do these changes affect your child?

You're experiencing these changes first. You're having a richer, more open personal experience of your own life while interacting with your child from that new place. Your child will feel it. Your child will "get" it. Your child will flourish as a result.

You'll notice your language, your wording and your tone of voice – even your movements and gestures – may have changed. You may be responding more effectively in stressful situations and relating better to various individuals in your life.

Remember how people noticed a change in me when my perspective changed?

With the child – and for those who care for and about them – mentorship will bring about a new kind of gentleness, comforting, and respectful manner, through a guiding, growth-oriented relationship.

Creating a Space for the Mentoring Experience

Earlier, I mentioned creating the mentoring experience in a psychologically safe environment. I found it to be important to separate my parenting from the mentoring until, at some later point, they blended together in harmony. I could only accomplish that as a result of my commitment to my *own* growth.

In my first experience, I created a special time to wear my mentoring "hat" separately from my parenting one. My goal was to have my son trust me, not fear me. At the first session, I sat with him and asked him to express anything that was on his mind. I wanted this experience to be different. I wanted him to feel he could be open with me.

He said, "I'm afraid if I do that, you'll hit me."

I assured him that this was a special time together – a sacred space – and that he could trust me and we could work out anything that was concerning him together.

Then he said, "You won't spank me like I see other Mommies do when I go to my friends' houses?"

I said, "No, I will not do that to you."

That was the real beginning of a bond of trust that we have to this day, fostered through everyday living.

What You Can Hope For:

Together with your child's own natural abilities, the knowledge you gain from this book, and the use of certain skills, strategies, and techniques, you'll be able to arm your children with tools that will connect them to their unique personal power and, ultimately, weave the foundation for their success.

Here's what you'll notice about yourself:

- How good it feels to naturally release any negativity and replace it with new, positive ideas and solutions.
- You're discovering and honoring your own deep values.
- You're developing a growing confidence about allowing your values to run your life, rather than allowing the media or others' opinions do it for you.
- You're learning how to create your own customized roadmap for the day, thereby preventing knee-jerk reactions to people and events.
- You're able to pin down productive actions that feel right, when you consistently work those inner muscles.
- You're beginning to experience *lasting*, positive change.

An important truism: You can't pull this off without a commitment to your own growth as a human being. It's easy because you'll *want* to do it, when you see results. You'll *feel* the changes.

I want to say here that many parents accomplish much without doing all the above but, oftentimes, the price is the wear and tear of the soul. Instead, this process provides you with a structure that helps you nourish *and* restore your soul through your own inner resources while crafting the life you want for yourself and your child.

You'll *want* to continue to feel empowered and also *to* empower. This will positively affect your relationships on every level of your life. You'll become a truly happy person!

What a concept!

I have a question for you: Is this the kind of parent you'd like your child to be reared by? Would you want them to ultimately become this kind of parent for *their* own children – for the next generation?

I hear a resounding "YES!"

Do you think this new parenting model, which rises to the occasion of our contemporary challenges by interfacing with the times we live in, will create fine men and women – and even leaders – to contribute to a better, advancing world?

I take my hat off to you for being on this journey with me.

By now, the work you've done has brought some visible, palpable improvements in not only *what* you feel, but in the way you interact with your child. This has prepared you for priceless new insights, skills, and knowledge, enabling you to go further than you may have thought possible with your parenting style. You're tapping deeper into a treasure that has always been there, patiently waiting to be accessed.

You're feeling good!

Along with this comes a growing feeling of personal fulfillment, extending itself into a wise parent; a role model to perpetuate this new parenting model for the next generation – empowering them to find and walk their own unique path.

Special Preface for Keys #5, #6 and #7

So – let's walk together as we look back on our journey, before beginning **Key #5**.

In Key #1, you saw that, in order to make a shift in your life, you needed to first make a shift in your perspective.

In Key #2, you've started to take action to make that shift by accessing your own true nature, which is really to live in the truth. You crave it, you want to align with it much in the same way a flower craves light in the process of photosynthesis.

Then something amazing happens: as you cultivate living in your truth as a natural way of life, you find you're automatically in harmony with the core values and basic truths that underlie what civilization represents and what we depend on to protect us.

You've expanded your awareness and consciousness by going both deeper *and* higher.

In Key #3, this new perspective you've developed automatically sets the stage for functioning on a more expansive level. This is supported by universal principles that, in the larger societal context, the most well-meaning among us strive to honor. Our basic inner work now leads us into the Values Zone. This relates to, and makes us aware of, the rights of others.

For example, The Golden Rule, "Do unto others as you would have them do unto you," is a universally accepted philosophical guideline for our behavior. However, if you don't have a balanced, appropriate sense of self-esteem and you haven't corrected it, you'll reflect that behavior. This gives you no platform from which to respect others and use The Golden Rule.

In contrast, getting in touch with your personal core values that you've now tapped intersects with the larger framework of universal values. You're aligned and you're ready to be the *best* version of you.

Can you imagine what the world could look like if everyone practiced the Golden Rule? By now, you might be able to see that you must wake up to your own magnificence in order to shape or recognize another's.

In Key #4, you built a framework for making parenting more conscious by becoming a mentor to your child. Your behavior now easily reflects your developing awareness, which will positively spill over to every relationship and naturally make you a much better parent and person.

This process is a wake-up call to change consciousness.

The remaining three **Keys – #5, #6** and **#7** – will reflect your own personal truths and path based on your unique religious affiliation and/or spiritual path, if any.

Because of that, they can't contain specific instructional material as I provided for you in the prior **Keys, #1** through **#4**. This is because customization has begun to take place.

Your life will have begun to reflect the specific guidance you've received from your own expanded awareness, or what is sometimes called the "higher self." You'll begin to experience a more enjoyable, self-directed life – automatically.

So now, **Keys #5, #6** and **#7** will explain both the concepts and benefits of these **Keys**, rather than specific additional steps required to achieve them.

• Key #5: Experiencing the Light: Life on a Brighter Level

Next, we're ready to enhance what you've already learned by adding a deeper dimension to it – the age-old concept of what is known as "*The Light*."

The word itself is not meant to imply any particular sectarian, religious, spiritual, or supernatural meaning. Instead, I just want to make use of a term people throughout history have repeatedly chosen to explain a recurring sense of something which, while difficult to put into words, seems best expressed by the idea of light; the expression of "radiance."

Many of us have encountered people who, by their mere presence, light up a room with a sense of radiance, almost a light. They uplift others while seeming to automatically bring a feeling of peace and healing. They inspire and motivate us, reversing negative situations, or simply enhancing an already positive event or environment.

You're beginning to experience a kind of radiance at this point in the process. This is the path you're moving into – one that allows you to both transform *and* to release negativity while experiencing more joy.

No two people will have the same experience. Regardless, the work – based on your commitment and personal characteristics – will improve many areas of your life.

You can find yourself in a state of momentum that comes from consistency and you may be starting to experience results. You might be able to notice that you're more easily avoiding being thrown off-track by the disruptions and stress of everyday life. This will help you to feel energized by the cumulative benefits of having added another vitally important daily habit of doing the practice. As a result, you're less likely to be dragged down to a lower level of functioning.

When I was a little girl, the carousel was my magical journey to the gold ring. I had a chance to catch one each time I completed a rotation of the carousel. That gold ring was, for me – as I'm sure it was for other children – the prize for getting out of the comfort zone, to reach beyond and experience the thrill of achievement.

I never forgot the thrill and magic of striving for the gold ring.

Among the "golden rings" that *you* might notice emerging from this new uplifted state are a strengthening of your intuitive and analytical skills and enhanced verbal and nonverbal communication abilities, helping you make right decisions.

Even decisions such as choosing the right school or the best health care for your child or for yourself are best handled by those who have integrated what's commonly referred to as the left *and* the right sides of the brain. As mentioned before, centering balances the left and right brain hemispheres, giving you access to better solutions.

What will show up naturally, as a result of this practice, are integrity, congruence, and an embodiment of the highest kinds of thoughts, feelings, and values. Based on your regularity of practice, you'll feel all of this on varying levels.

Other "golden rings" could include being able to release hostile feelings, to transform negativity, and to communicate and talk in ways that enable others to gain a different and higher perspective. You'll gain the ability to create and be attracted to healthy, win/win solutions.

Some of us will move more quickly into this state than others will. Give it some time, commitment and consistency. It *will* happen.

During a retreat I attended with a transformational teacher, the instructor said, "Once you open the window to transformation, you can never close it again." I agree with that statement.

Once you embark on the journey of self-discovery, you'll never be the same again, in that you can never *not* be the real you again. The journey itself brings about the destination. You've added new values and new truths, now fully articulated, all of which now reside in your new perspective and awareness. Your actions will now automatically be in harmony with your values. You've changed your life menu with new, improved choices.

Now you, as a person and parent, are blazing a new trail. Your child's development will be reflected and imprinted with new and creative ways to become a success. Those actions can and will affect the world around him or her.

The goal will be the experience of lasting, fundamental change elevating your life and the lives of those around you. This lasting change will foster your ability to make your full contribution to the world, as well as eliciting that ability from your child.

• Key #6: Living in the Light: Using and Sharing the Radiance

We're going to assume that you've grasped the material in **Keys #1** through **#5**. You now accept the concept of light/radiance as it applies to your unique nature and being. In other words, the dawning of the best version of who you can be in the world is already happening.

If you're not at this point yet – please go back through the process itself now so you can obtain the maximum benefit from the rest of the **Keys**.

It's now time to let your light shine in the outer world. You're ready now to know what you might expect to experience and how that would feel in terms of your everyday life.

Though each person's results will be unique to that particular individual, changes will be both felt and experienced externally. At the beginning, changes will start blending into your former ways of doing things. Your new insights may appear to be "spotty" but, in time, fundamental change *will* begin take root.

As I said earlier, at this stage in the process, you're beginning to experience a new kind of radiance. This is the path you're moving into – a path that allows you to transmute and shed negativity while experiencing more joy as you do so! As is dramatically demonstrated in the Olympics, you're passing the torch… of a new way of being – a new legacy – to your child. You are a light and you bring light to your offspring. Your children feel it in ways that are real in their everyday lives and that naturally become a part of who they are.

Now your child is reflecting what emerges from you and learns to handle situations in new ways. You've become a catalyst for your child's budding value system and you have a radiance that uplifts others, inspiring and motivating them to reverse or transform negativity by bringing light to it.

One way you transform negativity is by illuminating it. But, to bring the light, you have to *be* it, so that light can come through.

You're experiencing lasting, fundamental change. You've become like the Olympic torch relay runner. You've seen the starting of the Olympics, where they light the torch with the fire from Greece and then run it across the host country, blazing a new trail to the stadium, where the Olympic flame is waiting to be lit by the runner.

If you've gleaned what you need to do from the previous **Keys**, you've experiencing the fruit of your efforts. Using the analogy of physical fitness, where momentum allows you to get more physically fit, you're now able to reach higher states of thought and action to access richer solutions for those things that you want to change, by becoming fit with your mind and spirit.

As I've mentioned often – note that, with consistency, momentum builds. Now you – both as a person *and* as a parent – are blazing a new trail. Your child's development will be reflected and imprinted with new and creative ways to become a success. Those actions can and *will* affect the world around your children.

You've stepped into the new you and you see the real world in a different light.

Now you have a framework for your value system and the way you operate in the world. You know what you choose to do or not do and you're able to clearly decide between them. In other words, you not only feel the light around you, but you've learned how to *use* it.

That's exactly what the 21st century parenting method does for you. Now you're ready to direct that light and use it to build your relationship with your child and watch him or her flourish.

Again, to maintain the momentum of crafting our lives and building the spiritual wisdom muscles that stay strong, forming the foundation for a life we were meant to have, consistency is the key. It places you and **keeps** you in direct alignment with your values – the critical tools that are unique to you and that underlie what you're meant to become.

It's said that a pilot makes a minimum of 1000 manual adjustments during a flight to keep the plane from diverting from its scheduled destination. You are the pilot and CEO of your own life; *you* will be the one keeping *you* on track.

At the same time, you're standing in that light. You feel secure in your values and you begin to see all that you've learned is a gift that reveals itself in the actions you take.

What a gift! Why do I call it a gift? Because it gives you an opportunity to function in a way with yourself *and* with your child that wouldn't ordinarily have been available to you. This gift naturally manifests itself due to the infrastructure of your core beliefs and value system. The best news? It's yours to access, 24/7, for the rest of your life. I call that a real gift that you can give to your child and to yourself.

Nurturing your child's gift happens as you fulfill your own personal goals. That's what makes my method so unique. In essence, what you're doing now is using everything you've accomplished in the previous **Keys**. By being true to yourself, you're setting a wonderful example for your child.

As a good parent-mentor, you have the ability to make your own personal dreams come true and unlock your child's gift.

It was such a joy to see my child unfold into his own chosen destiny without the clutter of what could have been my own personal agenda. The process cleared me so I became a truer reflection for my son, allowing his own calling to flourish.

If you live a full life, you transfer that legacy to your child, who now has a role model to help fulfill his or her life. In unlocking your child's gift, what you discover is that, not only have you nourished yourself, but you've nourished your child at the same time – and you've done this easily and organically.

This is what being alive is about – that exciting "aha" moment that answers the question, "Why am I here?" You know you have something to give to your child and make the world better at the same time.

Isn't that what the world needs now?

George Bernard Shaw put it beautifully when he wrote, "Life is not a brief candle. It is a splendid torch that I want to make burn as brightly as possible before handing it on to future generations."

Our children are that generation and they can have their potential unlocked, to be the future leaders of our world.

Do you remember what my son answered, when I asked him if he smoked marijuana? He said, "Mom, I'm too high on life to do that!"

Arlene Karian

What kind of child would *you* like to bring up in this world?

I passed the torch to my child, and he's living the life of his dreams while making a contribution to other people's lives.

Now, it's your turn to pass the torch.

• Key #7: Automatic Cruise Control: Navigating Your Days with Joy and Ease

This **Key** enhances your ability to stay on track, because now you're choosing your intentions for the day, along with the qualities you want to express. You've tapped into the secret that you're the one who is crafting your life, along with the tools to manifest your personal, customized life path.

Our improved lives, which include our children enjoying this shared legacy, put us on automatic cruise control, where our higher functioning is automatically brought into the real world with a whole-brain/whole-mind fitness that integrates all of what we've accessed within ourselves. Your uplifted consciousness will be a catalyst to reach out and help others – including your child – to identify, express, and develop unique gifts and potential contributions to a world that's crying out for these gifts.

With consistent effort, you'll elicit authentic, values-based answers from your own consciousness, and experience the life-changing benefits.

All the steps are in action here as you go through your daily life, integrating the **Keys**, customizing and being in harmony with the traditions and religious and/or spiritual paths you choose. You'll notice that, to the extent you keep up your commitment to yourself, you'll consistently stay on track as you go through your day.

Reinforcement will keep you from being derailed, just as consistent results on the physical level bring their own kind of fitness: physical. In following this process, you'll be attaining mind-spirit fitness.

Your life is being lived from a place of automatic, unconscious competence. A sense of high functioning comes easily to you and you're enjoying the results.

Certainly, there will be ups and downs along the way – but you'll be more likely to access the resources needed to bounce back easily. And, you'll know where and how to find these resources quickly and easily.

Now, with consistency, you'll continue to develop these resources from within yourself. You can easily go back to the **Keys,** to instantly put yourself back on autopilot. If you require outside help, you'll have greater discernment by which to evaluate and choose those potential sources.

You'll enjoy a fuller, improved life. You'll also begin to notice that, as Einstein said, **"There are two ways to live: you can live as if nothing is a miracle; you can live as if everything is a miracle."** Living the latter way prepares you to make your full contribution to our world and to its betterment.

Imagine the deep significance your life will have when you strive to live it to its fullest!

Epilogue

There once was a man who wanted to find the meaning of life. "What is the meaning of life?" he pondered to himself for years. He became so obsessed with finding the answer that, one day, he gave up everything – job, family, and friends – to find the answer.

At the end of two years, having traveled all over the world, he found himself exhausted and tattered, pulling upon his last drop of energy to climb to the top of a Himalayan mountain. There, he was told, a guru would satisfy his desperate longing to find an answer.

When he reached the top, he saw the guru, sitting in a lotus position with his long, grey hair flowing in the wind. The man immediately bowed before him.

"Master," he said, "I have a question that has been burning within me and I am told you can answer it."

The guru said, "Ask, my child."

The man, with a dramatic gasp for breath, asked, "Master, what is the meaning of life?"

The guru reached out, put his hand over the man's head and, in a gesture of deep sanctity, answered, "My child, the meaning of Life? Life is a river!"

"A *river*?!" the man answered. "All this searching, divesting myself of anything material, giving up my family, my friends, my community, my *life* – and you're telling me that life is a *river*?"

The guru looked down at him, puzzled. He scratched his head and, after a long pause, said, "Well, what do you know? I *thought* it was a river. You mean it's *not*?"

What does this little story mean?

You don't have to travel.

You don't have to search for the meaning of life.

You don't have to ask anybody else!

You don't have to change your initials.

The answers are *inside!*

You will experience a level of joy and ease, because your answers are connected to your values.

You're experiencing the meaning of life daily, moment to moment, as your ideal existence – and you're enjoying the interchange of love between a parent and child in a new way.

You are a role model.

You are a mentor.

You are a light.

Meet Arlene Karian

Arlene Karian has had several careers – as a musician, writer, and successful entrepreneur – but her defining role is being the mother of an extraordinary son. When she struggled to survive financially as a divorced welfare mom, she vowed she would teach her son the critical life skills needed to overcome his challenges and make a contribution to society. She kept that promise.

"Mentoring is the new way," Arlene says. "I raised my son to excel while I was on welfare. It's because I blended parenting with mentoring that my son became so extraordinary, successful, and a living role model of my work. Helping all parents bring out the best in their children is now my passion."

Her eclectic background enabled Arlene to weave together several disciplines and create her unique life-enhancement system, the Road Map to 21st Century Parenting system she followed to mentor her son. She also developed a process that enabled her to start a rare coin business from scratch and build it into a million-dollar company.

Arlene is a sought-after speaker who has shared the podium with world-class leaders at the Pentagon, World Future Society, and the National Association for Women's Business Owners. As a published writer, her leading-edge articles have been featured in *Entrepreneur* magazine, *Whole Life Times* and other publications. An accomplished singer and pianist, Arlene has performed with the L.A. Opera and at New York's famous Town Hall. She lives in Florida.

Arlene has been blessed with the unique gift of blending the spiritual with the practical to bring about extraordinary results for her clients. *Mentoring Your Child To Win: The 7 Breakthrough Keys – How A Single, Former Welfare Mom Raised A Multi-Millionaire Kid* brings solutions for parenting in the 21st Century.

It is indeed a challenge to fully describe the nuances of inner growth and evolvement fully on the written page. For more information on mastering this system with private coaching, home study courses, and to receive regular updates and new discoveries as Arlene uncovers them, visit Arlene's Website at:

http://www.arlenekarian.com

Arlene Karian can be reached at:
(850) 622-3017 Office
(850) 586-1500 Cell
Email: lifepath@cox.net